These designs were all made using a ruler and doodles.

Add colour, then design your own on the blanks.

There are some ideas to help you.

Add make-up and jewellery.

Write things on.

Stick things on.

Good quality pencil crayons are recommended.

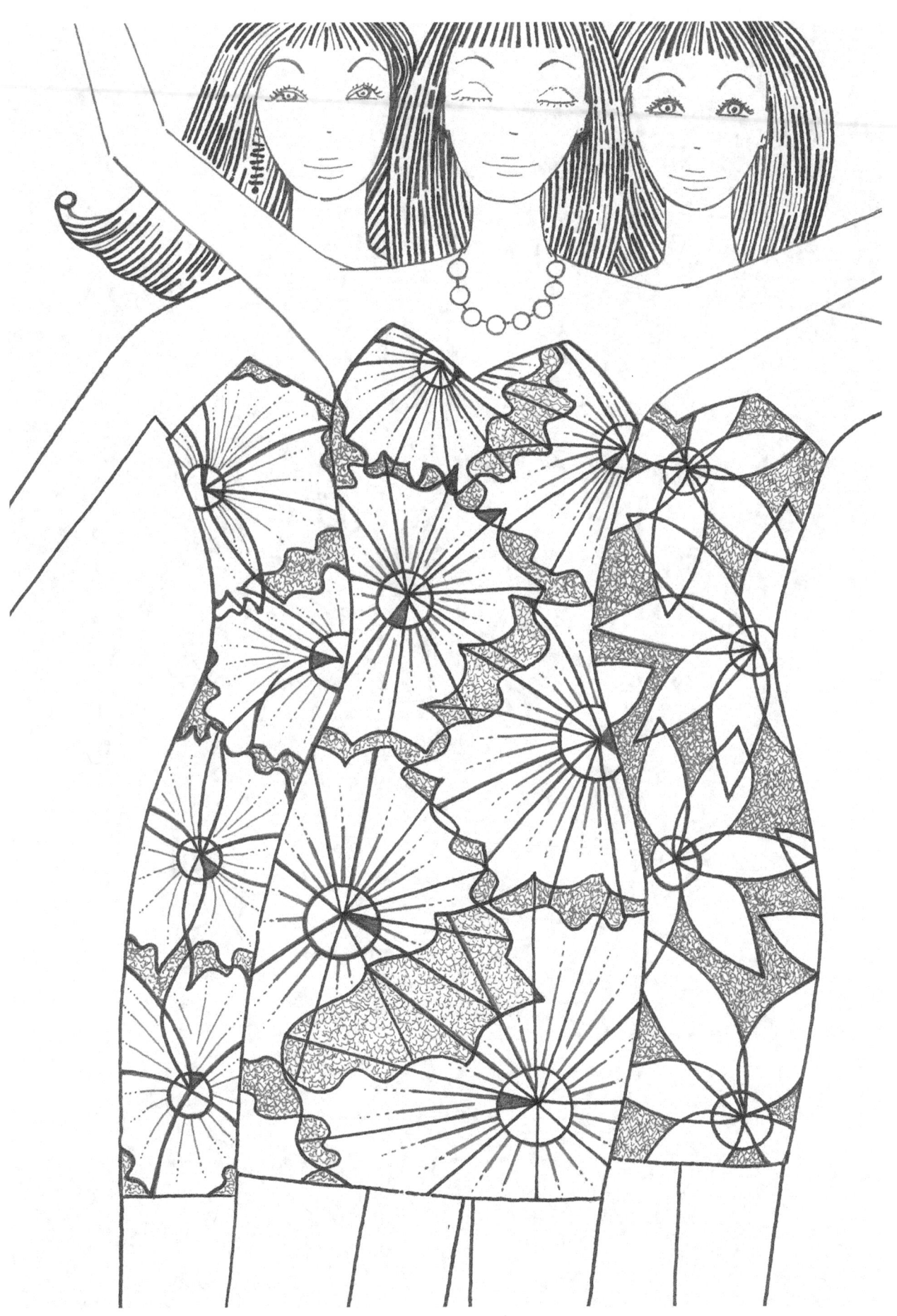

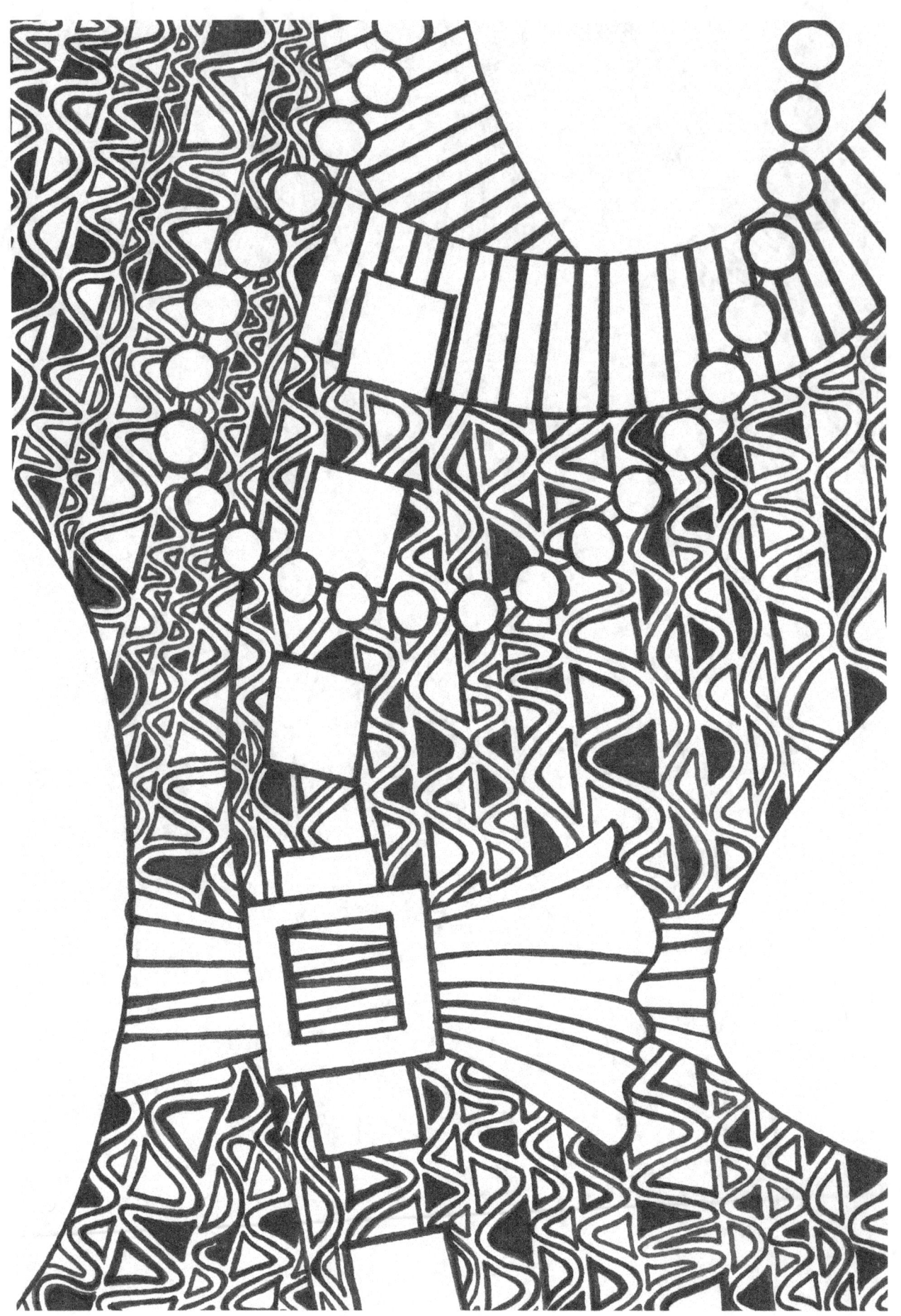

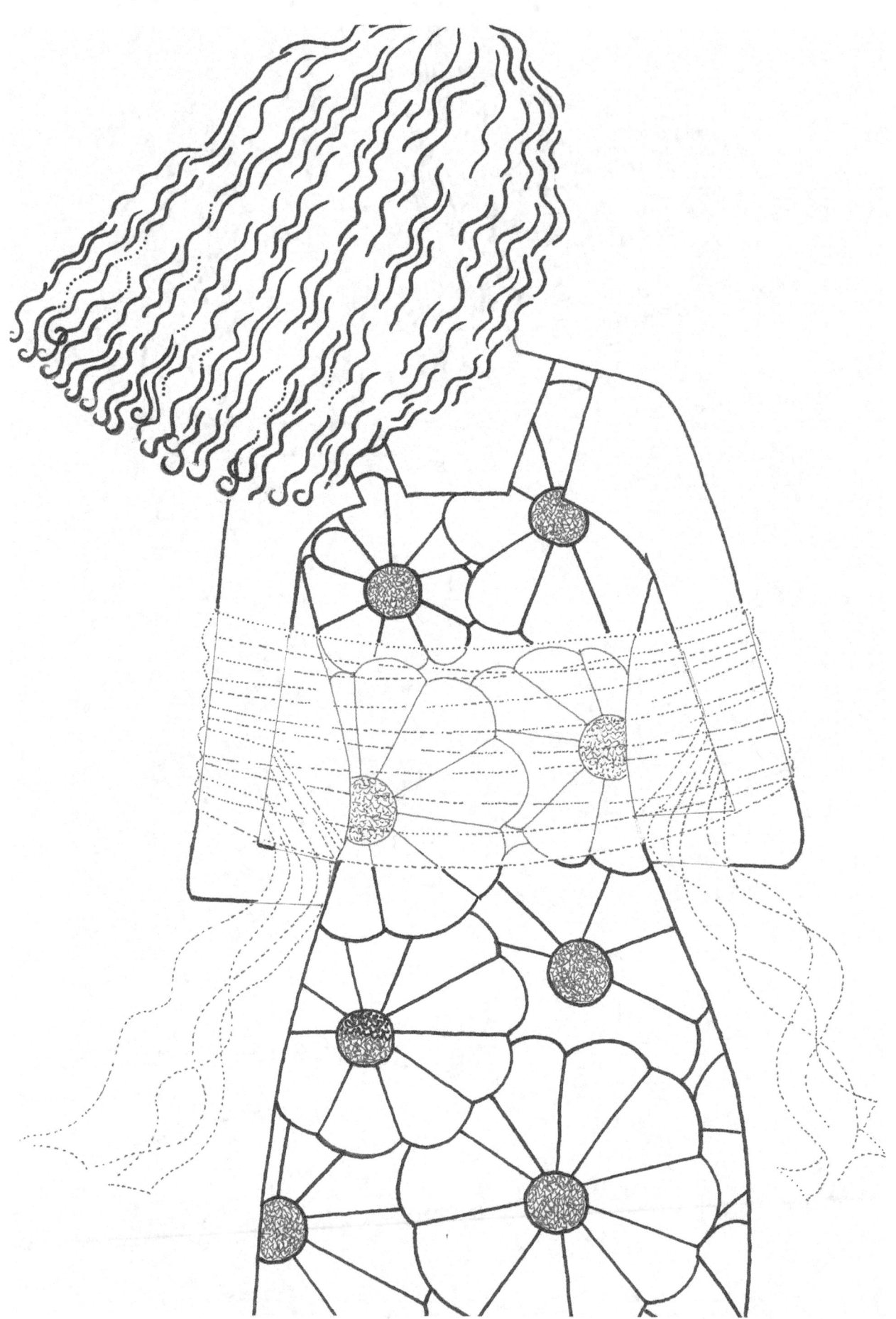

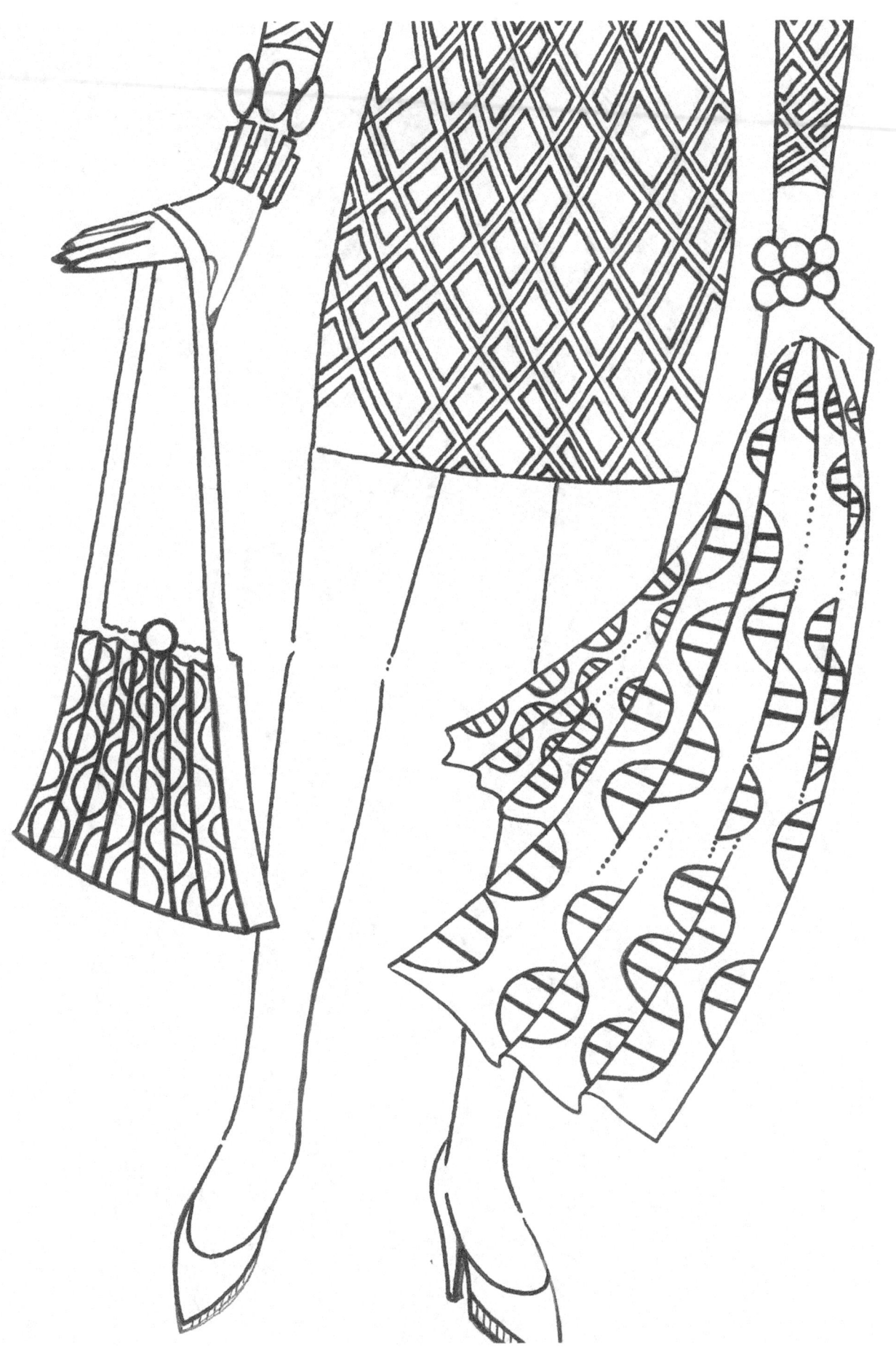

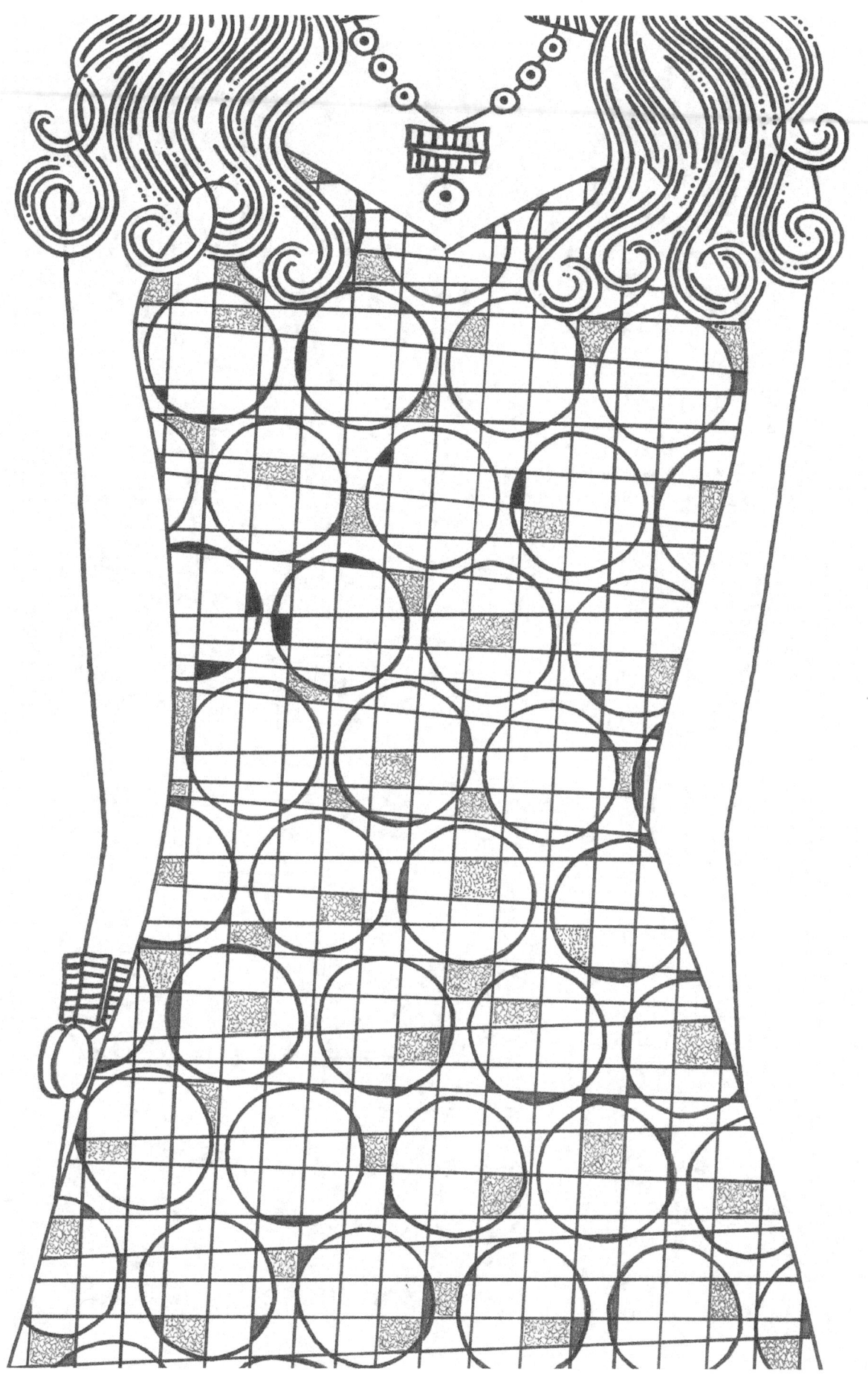

How to make patterns

How to make patterns

How to make patterns

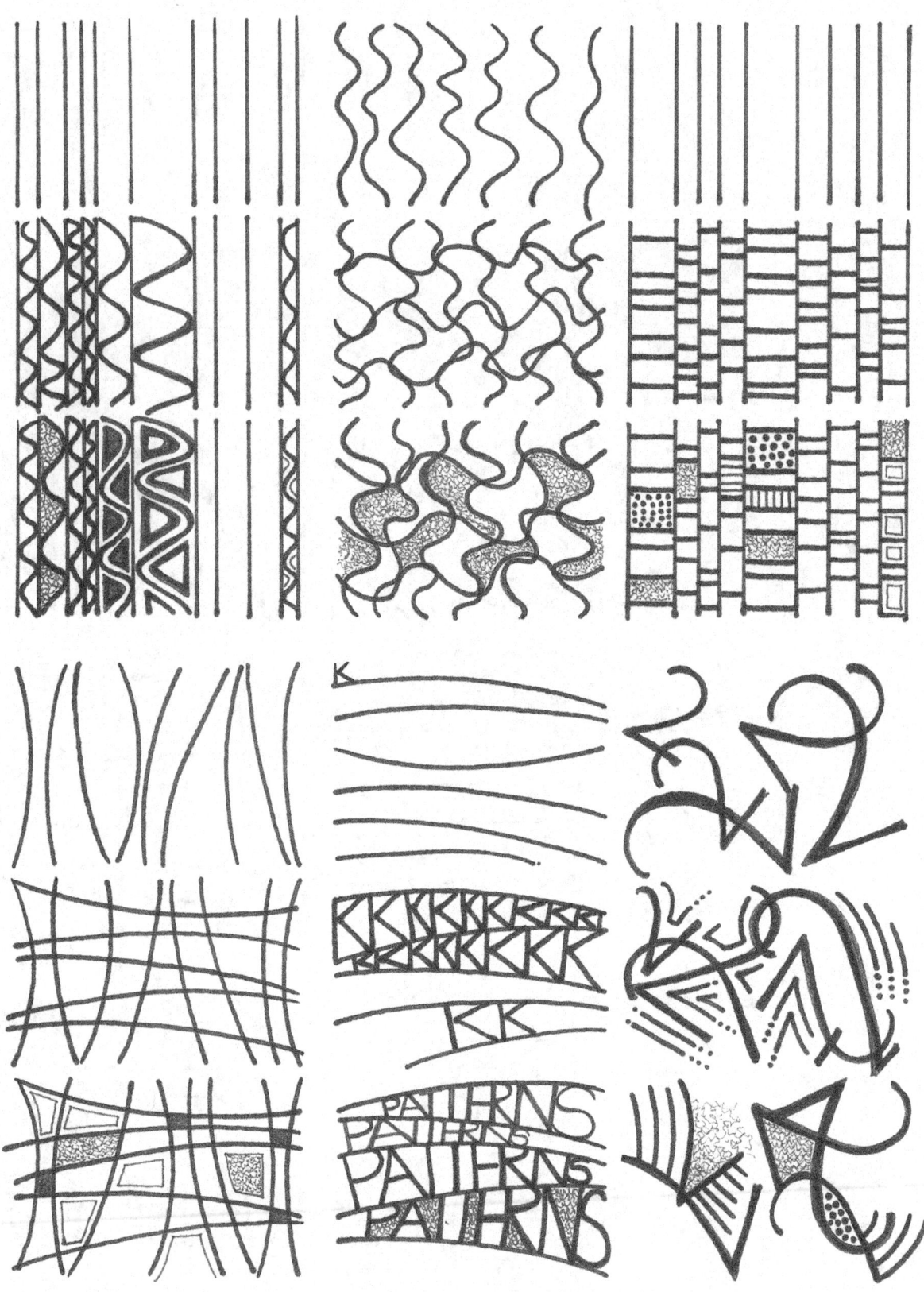

How to make patterns

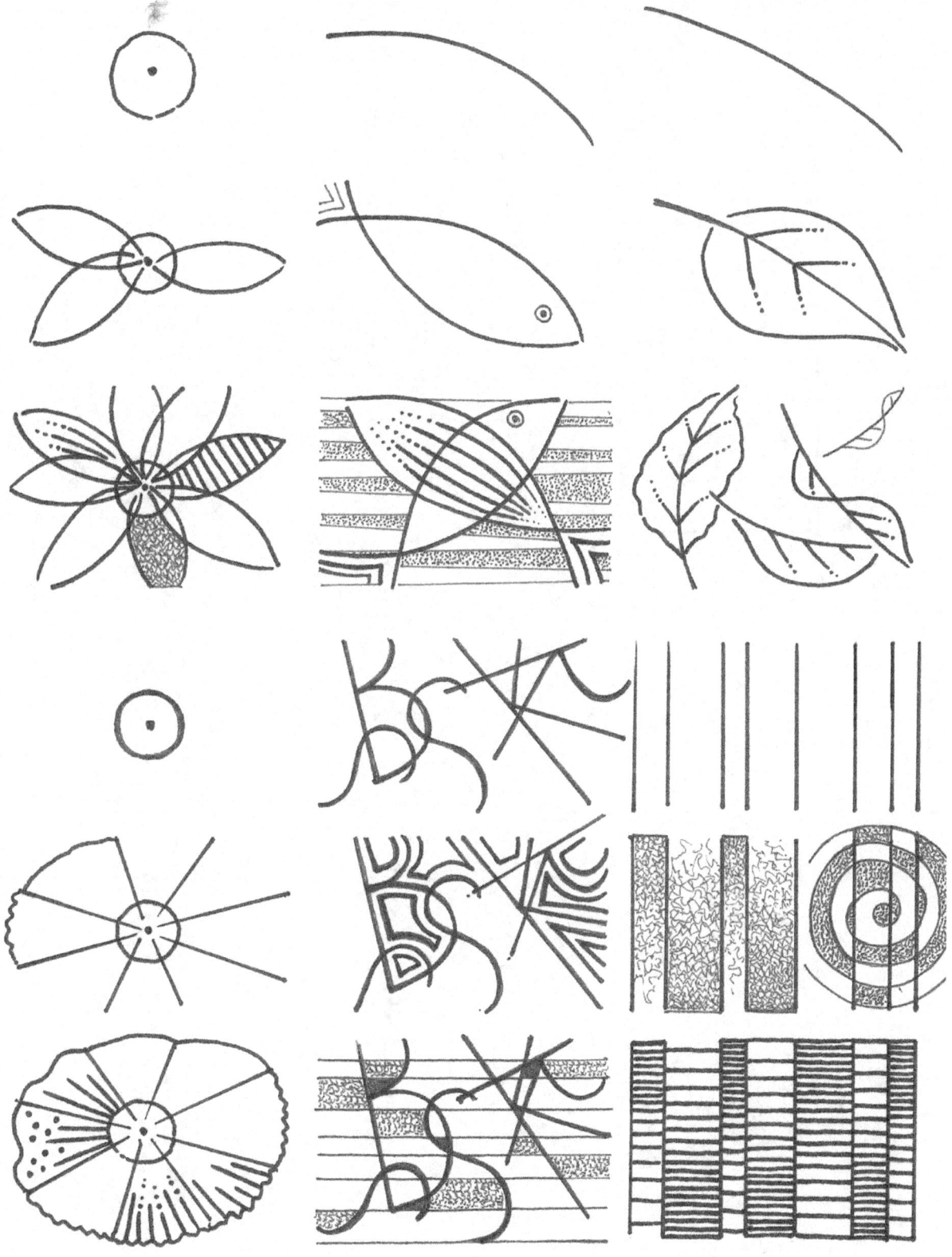

How to make patterns

How to make patterns

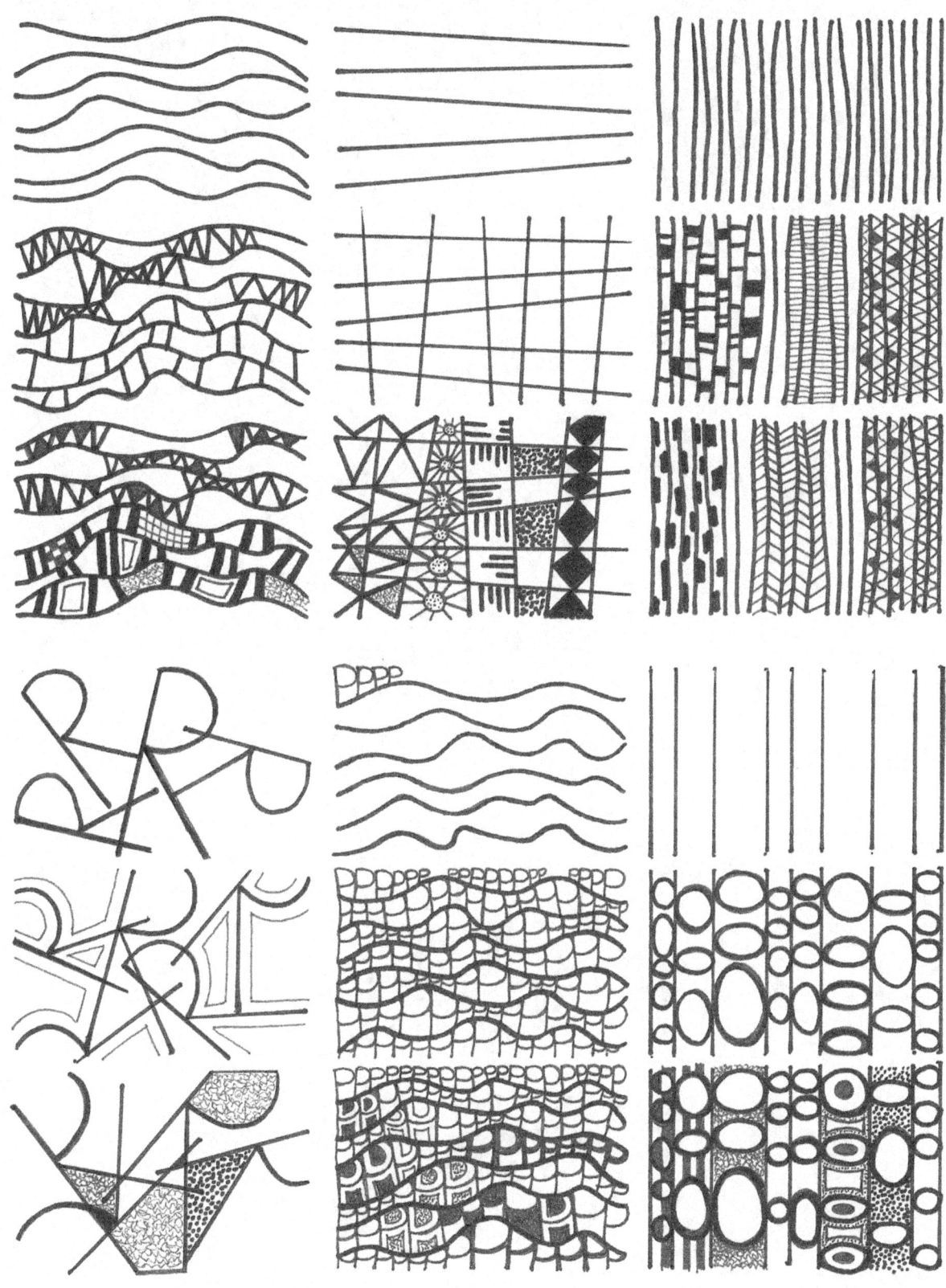

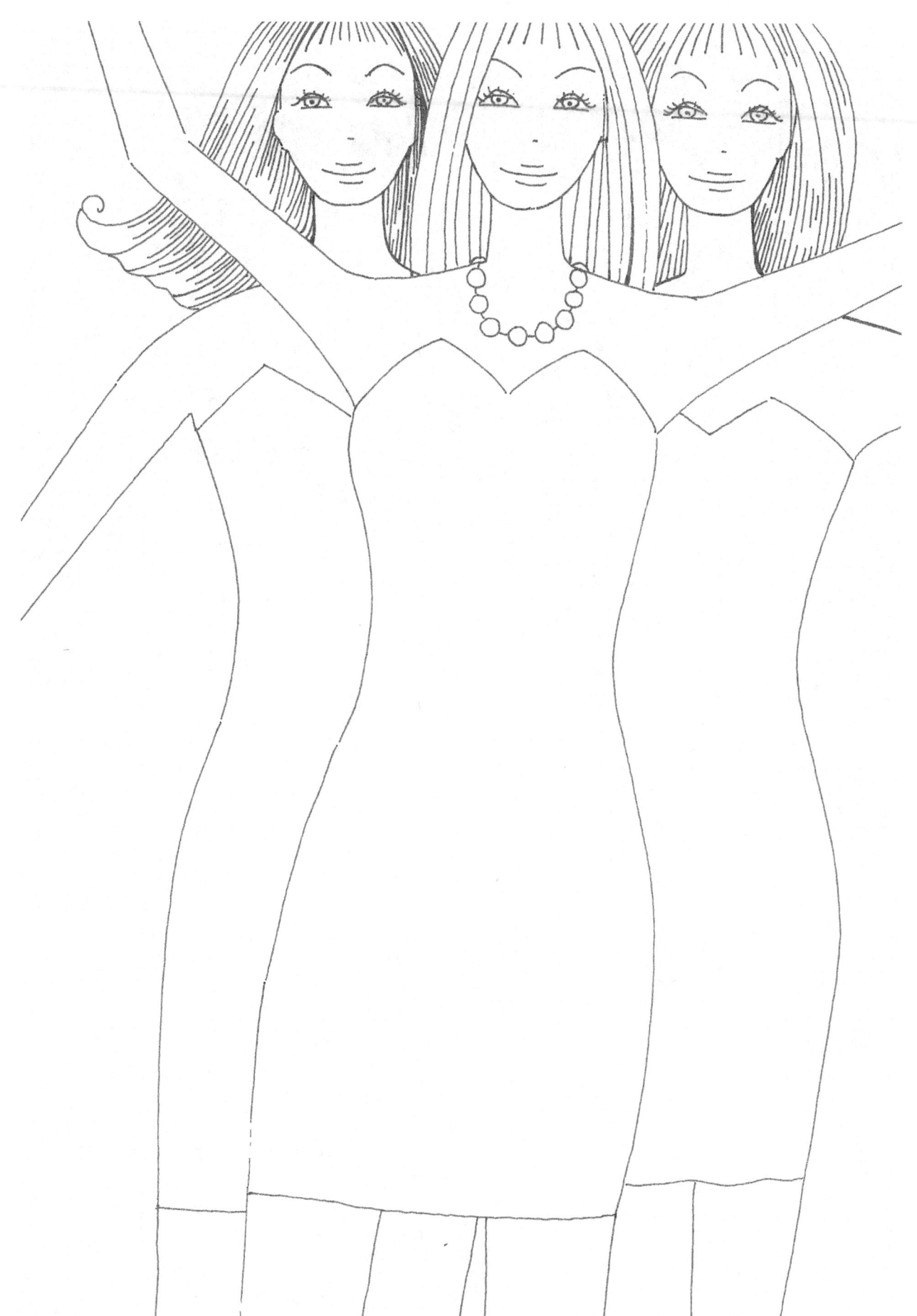

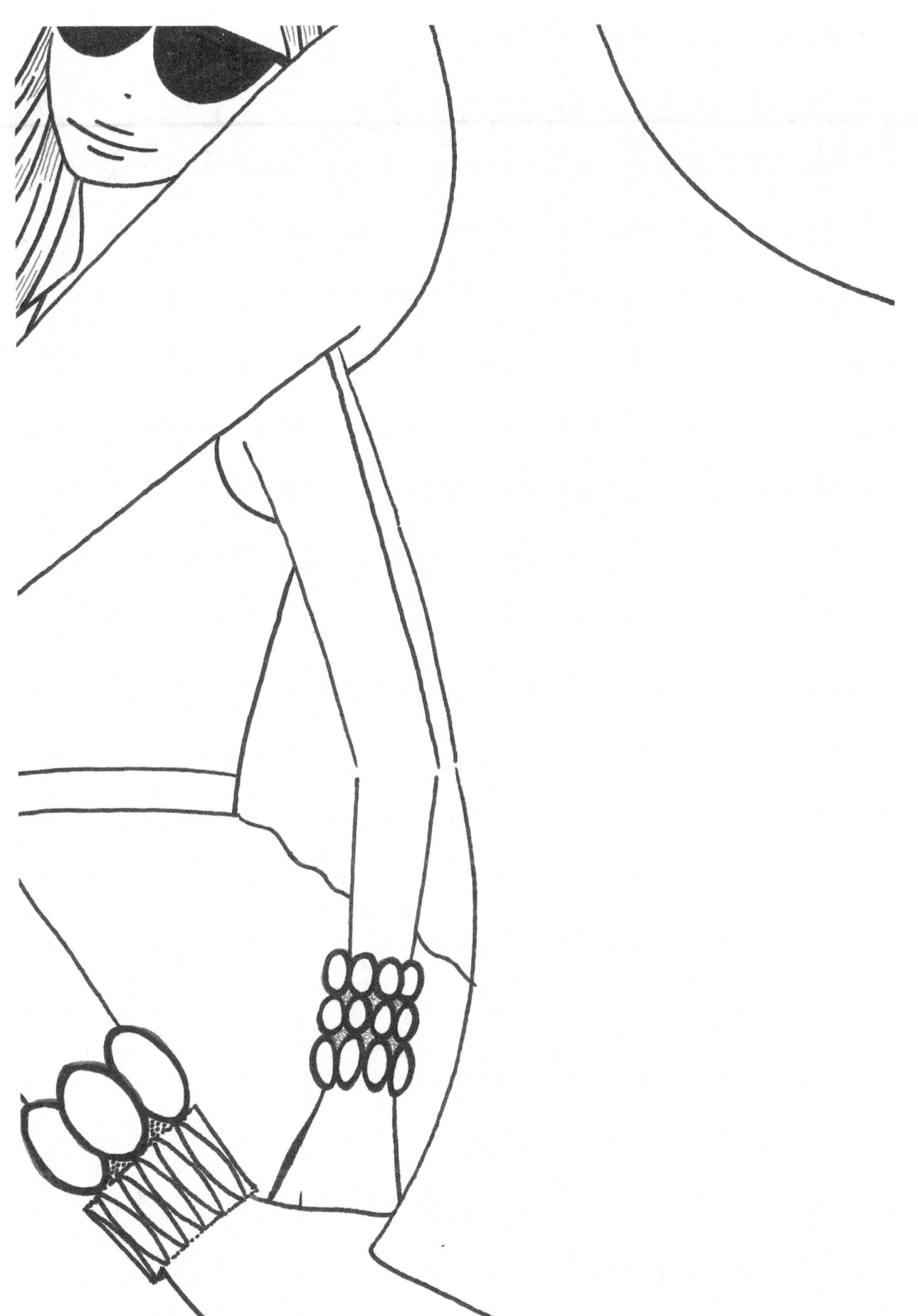